Dear Cara & Dora,

May you enjoy many years
together creating wonderful treats!

love,
Liz xxoo

holiday cupcakes

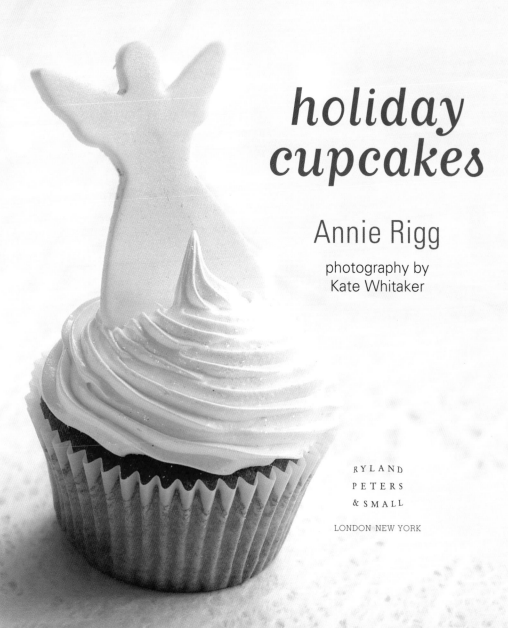

holiday
cupcakes

Annie Rigg

photography by
Kate Whitaker

RYLAND
PETERS
& SMALL

LONDON NEW YORK

Senior Designer Iona Hoyle
Senior Editor Céline Hughes
Head of Production Patricia Harrington
Art Director Leslie Harrington
Publishing Director Alison Starling

Prop Stylist Penny Markham
Indexer Penelope Kent

Author's acknowledgments
I would like to say another big thank you to
Kate Whitaker for her beautiful pictures and
to Penny Markham for her fabulous props.
Thanks also to Céline and Iona at Ryland Peters
& Small, for their patience and creativity in
putting together the whole package of words
and pictures in such a wonderful way.
And to my Mom, who is THE BEST.

First published in 2010.
This edition published in the US in 2011
by Ryland Peters & Small
519 Broadway, 5th Floor
New York, NY 10012
www.rylandpeters.com

10 9 8 7 6 5 4 3 2 1

Text © Annie Rigg 2010, 2011
Design and photographs
© Ryland Peters & Small 2010, 2011

Printed in China

ISBN: 978-1-84975-027-1

Library of Congress Cataloging-in-Publication
Data

Rigg, Annie.
 Holiday cupcakes / Annie Rigg ; photography
by Kate Whitaker.
   p. cm.
 Includes index.
 ISBN 978-1-84975-027-1
 1. Cupcakes. 2. Holiday cookery. I. Title.
 TX771.R56 2010
 641.5'68--dc22

                    2010014330

Notes
• All spoon measurements are level unless
otherwise specified.
• Eggs used in the recipes in this book are
large unless otherwise specified.
• Ovens should be preheated to the
specified temperatures. All ovens work
slightly differently. We recommend using
an oven thermometer and suggest you
consult the maker's handbook for any
special instructions, particularly if you
are cooking in a convection oven, as
you will need to adjust temperatures
according to manufacturer's instructions.

contents

time to celebrate!

At this time of year, you are likely to be incredibly busy, dashing around and preparing for the holidays. You may want to bake something special, either for a party or as a gift. But you can't face making a big cake or endless cookies. So what's the solution?

Cupcakes of course! It seems we just can't get enough of them.

Perfect for one, or made for sharing, cupcakes fit the bill no matter what the occasion. They make the perfect gift packaged into pretty boxes or when you want a dinky, sweet afternoon treat without going overboard on a great big slice of rich cake. Having said that you can, obviously, go completely over the top. Stockists of cupcake sprinkles and paper liners are now easy to find on the internet and any good kitchen store worth its salt will stock a selection of festive baking fancies with which to adorn and embellish your culinary creations.

All the recipes in this book make 12 regular-size cupcakes, which I find is just the right number to make, frost, and decorate in one sitting. However, I sometimes find that a recipe I have made umpteen times occasionally makes up to 16 cakes depending on the size of the paper liners used, which can vary enormously. The important thing to remember is to fill the liners no more than two-thirds full and they should be a success.

Some of the cakes are topped with full-on Christmas sparkle, while others simply incorporate the smells and flavors that you'd expect to come wafting out of the kitchen at this time of year. Toffee, chocolate, spices, dried fruit, and nuts are all here—and so are a few unexpected treasures. Candied Clementine with Pistachios on page 19

is one such example—clementines are a classic festive fruit but they are not often used as an ingredient in baking. Incorporated into this Spanish-inspired cupcake, you'll wonder why you haven't used them in cakes before. And whether you're entertaining in style, or feeding a horde of hungry children, you won't be stuck for ideas. The Gold & Silver Glitz cupcakes on page 23 are fit for royalty, and kids will fall in love with the hilarious Fat Penguins on page 27.

There's something here for everyone, whether you are a novice baker and are just starting out on a cupcake adventure or you are, like me, verging on the obsessed. Start with the simple and simply delicious Irish Cream cupcakes on page 16 and work your way up to the Christmas Ornaments on page 58, which are almost too pretty to eat.

Armed with a selection of food coloring pastes and a small number of piping tips and bags, there is no end to the delights that you can whip up at this most creative time of year. Take a look around you and feel inspired by the holiday season—just about anything works on top of an adorable cupcake.

basics

These are the basic cakes and frostings that are used in many recipes in this book. The cake recipes make 12–16 cupcakes, depending on the size of the paper liners you use. The frostings make enough to decorate the same number of cupcakes. You will need a candy thermometer for the Marshmallow Frosting and Meringue Buttercream.

buttermilk cake

12 tablespoons unsalted butter, softened

1 cup sugar

2 whole eggs and 1 egg yolk, beaten

1 teaspoon pure vanilla extract

1¾ cups all-purpose flour

1 teaspoon baking powder

½ teaspoon baking soda

½ cup buttermilk

Cream together the butter and sugar until light and creamy. Gradually add the beaten eggs, mixing well between each addition and scraping down the side of the mixing bowl from time to time. Add the vanilla. Sift together the flour, baking powder, and baking soda and add to the mixture in alternate batches with the buttermilk. Mix until smooth, then turn to the relevant recipe.

double chocolate cake

3 oz. bittersweet chocolate, chopped

3 tablespoons unsalted butter, softened

¾ cup packed light brown sugar

2 eggs, beaten

½ teaspoon pure vanilla extract

1 cup plus 2 tablespoons all-purpose flour

1 heaping tablespoon cocoa powder

½ teaspoon baking powder

1 teaspoon baking soda

a pinch of salt

½ cup sour cream

6 tablespoons boiling water

Melt the chocolate in a heatproof bowl over a pan of simmering water. Cream together the butter and sugar until light and creamy. Gradually add the beaten eggs, mixing well between each addition and scraping down the side of the mixing bowl from time to time. Add the vanilla and melted chocolate and stir well. Sift the flour, cocoa, baking powder, baking soda, and salt together. Add to the mixture in alternate batches with the sour cream. Add the boiling water and mix until smooth, then turn to the relevant recipe.

marshmallow frosting

1¼ cups sugar

1 tablespoon water

4 egg whites

a pinch of salt

Put all the ingredients in a heatproof bowl set over a pan of simmering water. Whisk slowly until the sugar has dissolved and the mixture is foamy. Continue cooking until the mixture reaches at least 140°F on a candy thermometer. Immediately pour the frosting into the bowl of a freestanding mixer fitted with the whisk attachment (or use an electric whisk and mixing bowl) and beat on medium speed until it will stand in stiff, glossy peaks—this will take about 3 minutes. Use immediately.

meringue buttercream

1 cup sugar

3 egg whites

2 sticks unsalted butter, softened and chopped

1 teaspoon pure vanilla extract

Put the sugar and egg whites in a heatproof bowl set over a pan of simmering water. Whisk until it reaches at least 140°F on a candy thermometer. Pour into the bowl of a freestanding electric mixer fitted with the whisk attachment (or use an electric whisk and mixing bowl). Beat until the mixture has doubled in volume, cooled, and will stand in stiff, glossy peaks—this will take about 3 minutes. Gradually add the butter to the cooled meringue mix, beating constantly, until the frosting is smooth. Fold in the vanilla and use immediately.

Chocolate variation:
Melt 5 oz. chopped bittersweet chocolate, then let cool slightly before stirring into the buttercream at the same time as the vanilla extract.

vanilla buttercream

3 sticks unsalted butter, softened

3 cups confectioners' sugar, sifted

a few drops of pure vanilla extract (optional)

Put the butter in a large bowl and, using a freestanding mixer or electric whisk, cream until really soft. Gradually add the sifted confectioners' sugar and beat until pale and smooth. Beat in the vanilla, if using.

simple

Coconut isn't necessarily associated with Christmas but these cakes, with their fluffy white frosting and scattering of coconut, really look like snowballs. Pipe the frosting into pointed swirls to look like snowy peaks instead of snowballs if you like.

coconut snowballs

1½ sticks unsalted butter, softened

1 cup sugar

3 eggs, beaten

1 teaspoon pure vanilla extract

1¾ cups all-purpose flour

1 teaspoon baking powder

½ teaspoon baking soda

a pinch of salt

½ cup desiccated coconut, plus extra to decorate

½ cup buttermilk, at room temperature

1 quantity Marshmallow Frosting (page 9)

1–2 muffin pans, lined with 12–16 paper cupcake liners

large piping bag, fitted with a plain tip

makes 12–16

Preheat the oven to 350°F.

Cream together the butter and sugar until pale and light. Gradually add the beaten eggs, mixing well between each addition and scraping down the bowl from time to time with a rubber spatula. Add the vanilla and mix again.

Sift together the flour, baking powder, baking soda, and salt. Stir in the desiccated coconut. Gradually add to the egg mixture in alternate batches with the buttermilk. Divide the mixture between the paper liners, filling them two-thirds full.

Bake on the middle shelf of the preheated oven for about 20 minutes, or until golden, well risen, and a skewer inserted into the middle of the cakes comes out clean. Remove from the oven and let cool in the pan for 5 minutes before transferring to a wire rack to cool completely.

Fill the piping bag with the Marshmallow Frosting and pipe generous swirls onto each cold cupcake. Dredge with lots of desiccated coconut.

Angels two ways! A fluffy angel food cake—ultra-light and made with egg whites—topped with a fondant- or royal-icing angel that's been lightly dusted with gold or silver luster. Heavenly. You will need to make the angels 2 days in advance.

angel cakes

confectioners' sugar, for dusting

8 oz. white ready-to-roll fondant or royal icing

gold and silver luster dusts

5 egg whites

a large pinch of cream of tartar

a pinch of salt

¾ cup plus 2 tablespoons superfine sugar

1 teaspoon pure vanilla extract

grated peel of ½ unwaxed lemon

½ cup plus 1 tablespoon all-purpose flour

1 quantity Marshmallow Frosting (page 9)

angel-shaped cookie cutter

1–2 muffin pans, lined with 12 paper cupcake liners

large piping bag, fitted with a large star tip

makes 12

Make the fondant/royal-icing angels 2 days before you make the cupcakes. Lightly dust a clean, dry work surface with confectioners' sugar. Roll the icing out to a thickness of no more than ¹⁄₁₆ inch. Using the angel cookie cutter, stamp out 12 angels. Set aside on baking parchment to dry out for 2 days.

When you are ready to make the cupcakes, preheat the oven to 350°F.

Brush gold and silver luster dusts over the angels.

Put the egg whites in the bowl of a freestanding mixer fitted with the whisk attachment (or use an electric whisk and a mixing bowl). Add the cream of tartar and salt and whisk until the egg whites just hold soft peaks. Gradually add the superfine sugar, beating well between each addition. Add the vanilla and lemon peel and fold in. Sift the flour into the bowl and fold in with a spatula or large metal spoon. Divide the mixture between the paper liners, filling them to the top.

Bake on the middle shelf of the preheated oven for 12–15 minutes, or until the cakes are golden and springy. Remove from the oven and let cool in the pan for 5 minutes before transferring to a wire rack to cool completely.

Fill the piping bag with the Marshmallow Frosting and pipe generous swirls onto each cold cupcake. Sprinkle with gold or silver luster dust and finish each cupcake with an angel.

Inside these cupcakes you'll find a triple dose of caramel and toffee—but somehow they're not overpoweringly sweet. With the final dazzle of spun sugar on top, they are the height of sophistication. Stay away if you're watching your weight!

salted caramel & toffee

1½ sticks unsalted butter, softened

½ cup sugar

½ cup dulce de leche

3 eggs, beaten

1 teaspoon pure vanilla extract

1⅛ cups all-purpose flour

3 teaspoons baking powder

a large pinch of salt

2–3 tablespoons milk

2½ oz. all-butter toffees, chopped

salted caramel frosting

¾ cup sugar

⅔ cup heavy cream

a large pinch of sea salt flakes

14 tablespoons unsalted butter, softened

spun sugar

¾ cup sugar

1–2 muffin pans, lined with 12 paper cupcake liners

large piping bag, fitted with a large star tip

makes 12

Preheat the oven to 350°F.

Cream together the butter and sugar until pale and light. Stir in the dulce de leche. Gradually add the beaten eggs, mixing well between each addition and scraping down the bowl from time to time with a rubber spatula. Add the vanilla and mix again. Sift together the flour, baking powder, and salt. Add to the egg mixture, with the milk, and mix until smooth. Divide the mixture between the paper liners, filling them two-thirds full, then scatter the toffees over the top. Bake on the middle shelf of the preheated oven for 20 minutes, or until well risen and a skewer inserted into the middle of the cakes comes out clean. Remove from the oven and let cool in the pan for 5 minutes before transferring to a wire rack to cool completely.

To make the salted caramel frosting, put the sugar in a small, heavy-based saucepan with 1 tablespoon water over low heat. Dissolve the sugar, without stirring. Raise the heat and cook until the sugar is a deep amber color. Remove from the heat and add the cream and salt. The caramel will bubble furiously and harden but stir to melt it into the cream. Let cool. Beat the butter until fluffy, gradually add to the cold caramel, and beat until smooth. Fill the piping bag with the frosting and pipe swirls onto each cold cupcake.

To make the spun sugar, put the sugar in a small, heavy-based saucepan with 1 tablespoon water over low heat until dissolved. Remove from the heat and let cool slightly. Drizzle the caramel over the bottom of an upturned greased bowl, let harden for 10 seconds, then break into pieces and arrange on top of each cupcake.

This rich, dark, and slightly smoky-tasting cupcake is topped with a delicately flavored Irish cream frosting. The unfrosted cakes keep really well in an airtight container and can be made a couple of days before you plan to serve them.

irish cream

¾ cup Guinness or other stout

1½ sticks unsalted butter, diced

⅓ cup cocoa powder, sifted

1¼ cups sugar

3 tablespoons sour cream

1 egg

1 egg yolk

1 teaspoon pure vanilla extract

1⅔ cups all-purpose flour

1½ teaspoons baking soda

a pinch of salt

edible silver balls

irish cream frosting

1½ cups mascarpone

3 tablespoons confectioners' sugar

¼ cup Baileys Irish Cream liqueur

1–2 muffin pans, lined with 12–16 paper cupcake liners

makes 12–16

Preheat the oven to 350°F.

Put the Guinness and butter in a small saucepan over low-medium heat. Leave until the butter has melted, then bring to a simmer. Remove from the heat, pour into a large bowl, and let cool.

Add the cocoa and sugar to the Guinness mixture and beat until smooth. In another bowl, whisk together the sour cream, whole egg, egg yolk, and vanilla. Add to the Guinness mixture and whisk until smooth. Sift together the flour, baking soda, and salt and add to the egg mixture. Whisk until smooth.

Transfer the mixture to a small pitcher and pour into the paper liners, filling them two-thirds full. Bake on the middle shelf of the preheated oven for about 15–20 minutes, until well risen and a skewer inserted into the middle of the cakes comes out clean. Remove from the oven and let cool in the pan for 5 minutes before transferring to a wire rack to cool completely.

To make the Irish cream frosting, beat together the mascarpone, sugar, and Baileys until smooth. Spread generously onto each cold cupcake. Scatter with edible silver balls and serve.

Prepare the crystallized clementine peel at least 6 hours before you plan to serve these cakes so that they have time to dry out. I have embellished the finished cakes with a festive flutter of edible gold leaf but feel free to leave this out.

candied clementine
with pistachios

2 clementines

3 eggs

¾ cup sugar

1 cup plus 2 tablespoons all-purpose flour, plus extra for dusting

2 teaspoons baking powder

a pinch of salt

½ cup ground almonds

⅓ cup unsalted, shelled pistachios, finely chopped

crystallized clementine peel

3 clementines

½ cup sugar

to decorate

1 cup confectioners' sugar

⅓ cup unsalted, shelled pistachios, chopped

edible gold leaf

1–2 muffin pans

makes 12–16

To make the crystallized clementine peel, pare the peel from the clementines using a vegetable peeler and cut into shreds. (Reserve the peeled clementines for the icing.) Mix the shreds and sugar on a baking sheet and set aside, uncovered, for at least 6 hours.

When you are ready to make the cupcakes, put the 2 (unpeeled) clementines in a saucepan. Cover with water, bring to a boil, and simmer gently for about 1 hour, or until tender. Drain and let cool. Preheat the oven to 350°F. Grease the insides of the muffin pan, lightly dust with all-purpose flour, and tip out the excess.

Quarter the cooked clementines and remove any pips. Purée the fruit (peel and all) in a food processor until nearly smooth. Put the eggs and sugar in the bowl of a freestanding mixer fitted with the whisk attachment (or use an electric whisk and a mixing bowl). Whisk until doubled in volume and very pale and thick. Sift together the flour, baking powder, and salt and fold into the egg mixture. Add the almonds, pistachios, and puréed clementines and fold in. Pour the mixture into the prepared pan, filling the holes to the top. Bake on the middle shelf of the preheated oven for about 15 minutes, or until well risen and a skewer inserted into the middle of the cakes comes out clean. Remove from the oven and let cool in the pan for 5 minutes. Run a knife around the cupcakes and pop them out onto a wire rack to cool.

To decorate, squeeze the juice from the reserved clementines. Sift the sugar into a bowl and add enough juice so that the icing just runs off the sides of the cakes. Spoon over each cake and let set before garnishing with the crystallized peel, pistachios, and bits of gold leaf.

simple 19

White chocolate and cranberries are a mouthwatering combination, and perfect during the Christmas season. Try to master the chocolate flakes for the topping because they finish off the cakes beautifully.

white chocolate
with cranberries

10 tablespoons unsalted butter, softened

¾ cup plus 2 tablespoons sugar

2 eggs, beaten

1 teaspoon pure vanilla extract

1⅓ cups all-purpose flour, plus extra for dusting

1 teaspoon baking powder

½ teaspoon baking soda

a pinch of salt

3 tablespoons sour cream or milk, at room temperature

⅔ cup white chocolate chips

½ cup dried cranberries

1 quantity Meringue Buttercream (page 9)

white chocolate, shaved with a vegetable peeler

red sugar-coated candies

1–2 muffin pans, lined with 12–16 red cupcake liners

makes 12–16

Preheat the oven to 350°F.

Cream together the butter and sugar until pale and light. Gradually add the beaten eggs, mixing well between each addition and scraping down the bowl from time to time with a rubber spatula. Add the vanilla and mix again.

Sift together the flour, baking powder, baking soda, and salt. Add to the egg mixture and mix again for 10 seconds. Add the sour cream or milk and mix again until smooth.

Put the chocolate chips and cranberries in a separate bowl and toss with about 1 tablespoon all-purpose flour. This will help prevent them from sinking to the bottom of the cupcakes when they're baked. Stir the chocolate chips and cranberries into the cupcake mixture. Divide the mixture between the paper liners, filling them two-thirds full.

Bake on the middle shelf of the preheated oven for 20 minutes, or until golden, well risen, and a skewer inserted into the middle of the cakes comes out clean. Remove from the oven and let cool in the pan for 5 minutes before transferring to a wire rack to cool completely.

Spread the Meringue Buttercream generously onto each cold cupcake. Top with white chocolate curls and a few red sugar-coated candies.

Perfect if you want something simple, elegant, and ever so slightly decadent, these cupcakes are just as fabulous served at a special occasion, such as birthdays or wedding anniversaries, as they are at Christmas.

gold & silver glitz

1 quantity Buttermilk Cake
(page 8)

1 quantity Marshmallow Frosting
(page 9)

gold and silver luster dusts

edible gold and silver balls

little white sugar flowers

*1–2 muffin pans,
lined with 12 gold and silver
cupcake liners*

*large piping bag,
fitted with a large star tip*

makes 12

Preheat the oven to 350°F.

Divide the Buttermilk Cake between the cupcake liners, filling them two-thirds full.

Bake on the middle shelf of the preheated oven for about 20 minutes, or until golden, well risen, and a skewer inserted into the middle of the cakes comes out clean. Remove from the oven and let cool in the pan for 5 minutes before transferring to a wire rack to cool completely.

Fill the piping bag with the Marshmallow Frosting and pipe swirls onto each cold cupcake, zigzagging the frosting from side to side and piling it up. Finish with a little flourish at the top.

Generously decorate each cupcake with a selection of luster dusts and gold and silver balls and finish by gently pushing a couple of little white sugar flowers into the frosting on each cupcake.

This moist, spicy cake is topped with a mountain of meringue buttercream delicately flavored with cinnamon and studded with stem ginger—perfect on a cold winter's afternoon with a steaming mug of tea.

sticky gingerbread

1½ sticks unsalted butter, softened

½ cup packed light brown sugar

3 tablespoons dark molasses

3 eggs, beaten

1⅛ cups all-purpose flour

3 teaspoons baking powder

2½ teaspoons ground ginger

1 teaspoon ground cinnamon

¼ teaspoon ground allspice

¼ teaspoon ground nutmeg

a pinch of salt

2–3 tablespoons milk

1 quantity Meringue Buttercream (page 9) but made with ½ teaspoon ground cinnamon instead of the vanilla extract

2 tablespoons chopped stem ginger in syrup

1–2 muffin pans, lined with 12 paper cupcake liners

large piping bag, fitted with a plain tip

makes 12

Preheat the oven to 350°F.

Cream together the butter, sugar, and molasses until light and fluffy. Gradually add the beaten eggs, mixing well between each addition and scraping down the bowl from time to time with a rubber spatula.

Sift together the flour, baking powder, spices, and salt. Gradually add to the egg mixture with the milk. Divide the mixture between the paper liners, filling them two-thirds full.

Bake on the middle shelf of the preheated oven for about 20 minutes, or until well risen and a skewer inserted into the middle of the cakes comes out clean. Remove from the oven and let cool in the pan for 5 minutes before transferring to a wire rack to cool completely.

Fill the piping bag with the cinnamon-flavored Meringue Buttercream and pipe generous swirls onto each cold cupcake. Scatter the chopped stem ginger around the frosting.

cute

You can't make a cuter cupcake than this. Adults will love them just as much as kids, so set aside a fun afternoon to create these adorable little characters. Complete the wintry scene with crushed meringues scattered around the penguins.

fat penguins

1 quantity Buttermilk Cake
(page 8)

1 quantity Vanilla Buttercream
(page 9)

black food coloring paste

tiny white chocolate drops

4 oz. white ready-to-roll
fondant icing

yellow food coloring paste

red food coloring paste

*muffin pan, lined with
8–10 paper cupcake liners*

*mini-muffin pan, lined with
8–10 paper liners in the
coordinating size*

makes 8–10

Preheat the oven to 350°F.

Divide the Buttermilk Cake between the paper liners, filling them two-thirds full. Bake on the middle shelf of the preheated oven for 12–25 minutes, depending on the size of the cakes—take them out when they are well risen and a skewer inserted into the middle of the cakes comes out clean. Remove from the oven and let cool in the pan for 5 minutes before transferring to a wire rack to cool completely.

Put two-thirds of the Vanilla Buttercream in a bowl and tint it black using the food coloring paste. Remove the paper liners from all the cold cakes and trim the top off each cake to make it level. Lay the larger cupcakes upside down and dab a little buttercream on the top. Lay a mini-muffin upside down on top of each larger cupcake. Spread black buttercream all over the penguins, leaving the area for the tummy unfrosted. Spread untinted buttercream into the tummy area. Press 2 white chocolate drops onto each penguin's face for the eyes. Dab a little black food coloring onto the middle of each eye.

Take 2 tablespoons of the fondant icing and tint it yellow. Break off small nuggets of the icing and shape into triangles for the beaks. Stick one onto each penguin. Color half of the remaining icing black. Pinch off hazelnut-size pieces and shape and flatten into wings. Press one wing onto either side of each penguin. Use the remaining icing to make the ski caps. Tint three-quarters of it red and leave the remainder white. Roll and pinch the red icing into cones and bend the ends so that they droop. Roll the white icing into small balls and stick to the end of each cap. Carefully place a cap on top of each penguin.

These chocolatey red velvet cupcakes are topped with minty meringue buttercream, marbled red and white to match and complement the stripy candy canes perched on the top.

candy canes

1 quantity Meringue Buttercream (page 9) but made with peppermint extract instead of vanilla

12 small candy canes

red velvet cupcakes

1½ sticks unsalted butter, softened

¾ cup plus 2 tablespoons sugar

2 eggs, beaten

1 teaspoon pure vanilla extract

red food coloring paste (ruby or Christmas red)

1⅓ cups all-purpose flour

2 tablespoons cocoa powder

a pinch of salt

½ cup buttermilk, at room temperature

1 teaspoon baking soda

1 teaspoon white wine vinegar

1–2 muffin pans, lined with 12 striped paper cupcake liners

large piping bag, fitted with a large star tip

makes 12

Preheat the oven to 350°F.

To make the red velvet cupcakes, cream together the butter and sugar until pale and light. Gradually add the beaten eggs, mixing well between each addition and scraping down the bowl from time to time with a rubber spatula. Add the vanilla and ½ teaspoon of the food coloring paste and mix until thoroughly incorporated.

Sift together the flour, cocoa, and salt. Gradually add to the egg mixture in alternate batches with the buttermilk.

In a small bowl, mix together the baking soda and vinegar. Add to the cake mixture and mix again until smooth. Divide the mixture between the paper liners, filling them two-thirds full.

Bake on the middle shelf of the preheated oven for about 20 minutes, or until well risen and a skewer inserted into the middle of the cakes comes out clean. Remove from the oven and let cool in the pan for 5 minutes before transferring to a wire rack to cool completely.

Divide the peppermint Meringue Buttercream between two bowls and tint one red using the food coloring paste. Using a large metal spoon, very lightly stir one color into the other so that they become marbled. Fill the piping bag with the frosting and pipe swirls onto each cold cupcake. Top with a candy cane.

These simple cupcakes are topped with a selection of sparkling mini-baubles in festive colors. Make them in a variety of sizes and colors for the prettiest effect.

glitter baubles

11 oz. white ready-to-roll fondant or royal icing

assorted food coloring pastes

assorted edible glitters and luster dusts

1 quantity Buttermilk Cake (page 8)

1 quantity Vanilla Buttercream (page 9)

1–2 muffin pans, lined with 12 silver cupcake liners

makes 12

Make the fondant/royal-icing baubles 2 days before you make the cupcakes. Using the assorted food coloring pastes, tint the icing in different colors. Roll into mini-baubles of different sizes. Dust the baubles in glitter and/or brush with luster dust. Set aside on baking parchment to dry out for 2 days.

When you are ready to make the cupcakes, preheat the oven to 350°F.

Divide the Buttermilk Cake between the cupcake liners, filling them two-thirds full.

Bake on the middle shelf of the preheated oven for about 20 minutes, or until golden, well risen, and a skewer inserted into the middle of the cakes comes out clean. Remove from the oven and let cool in the pan for 5 minutes before transferring to a wire rack to cool completely.

Spread the Vanilla Buttercream generously onto each cold cupcake. Arrange the mini-baubles on top.

Here's a forest of sparkly, festively adorned trees topped with silver and gold stars. All they need now is a pile of gifts underneath them...You'll need to be reasonably confident with a piping bag for these, but practice makes perfect!

christmas trees

1 quantity Buttermilk Cake
(page 8)

1 quantity Meringue
Buttercream (page 9)

green food coloring paste

edible green glitter

colored sugar balls

gold and silver sugar stars

*1–2 muffin pans, lined with
12 brown paper cupcake liners*

*large piping bag,
fitted with a medium star tip*

makes 12

Preheat the oven to 350°F.

Divide the Buttermilk Cake between the cupcake liners, filling them two-thirds full.

Bake on the middle shelf of the preheated oven for about 20 minutes, or until golden, well risen, and a skewer inserted into the middle of the cakes comes out clean. Remove from the oven and let cool in the pan for 5 minutes before transferring to a wire rack to cool completely.

Put three-quarters of the Meringue Buttercream in a bowl and tint it green using the food coloring paste. Leave the rest untinted and spread some of this over the top of each cold cupcake.

Fill the piping bag with the green frosting and, working from the center, pipe pointed branch shapes towards the edges of the cupcake. Keep doing this, turning the cupcake as you go, until you have the bottom of a tree. Repeat with the next layer up, making the branches shorter. Carry on with more layers, making the branches ever shorter as you get to the top of the tree.

Dust with green glitter and decorate with colored sugar balls. Top with a gold or silver star.

These fantastic little Santas are guaranteed to bring a smile to your face. They're great fun to make and would be a welcome addition to any Christmas party!

little santas

all-purpose flour, for dusting

1 quantity Buttermilk or Double Chocolate Cake (page 8)

1 lb. white ready-to-roll fondant or royal icing

red food coloring paste

confectioners' sugar, for dusting

12 tablespoons apricot jam

12 waffle cones

1 quantity Meringue Buttercream (page 9)

black food coloring paste

1–2 muffin pans

3-inch round cookie cutter

large piping bag, fitted with a medium star tip

makes 12

Preheat the oven to 350°F. Grease the insides of the muffin pan, lightly dust with all-purpose flour, and tip out the excess. Pour the Buttermilk or Double Chocolate Cake into the prepared muffin pan, filling the holes two-thirds full. Bake on the middle shelf of the preheated oven for about 20 minutes, or until well risen and a skewer inserted into the middle of the cakes comes out clean. Remove from the oven and let cool in the pan for 5 minutes. Run a knife around the cupcakes and pop them out onto a wire rack to cool.

Tint three-quarters of the fondant/royal icing red using the food coloring paste. Lightly dust a clean, dry work surface with confectioners' sugar. Roll the icing out to a thickness of ¹⁄₁₆ inch. Cut into 12 triangles to fit around the waffle cones. Warm the jam in a small saucepan, sieve it, then brush the outsides of the waffle cones in a thin layer. Cover each cone with the red icing, smoothing into place with your hands. Trim off any excess.

Take about 2½ oz. of the remaining icing and tint it pale pink with a tiny dot of red food coloring. Roll this out thinly and stamp out 12 x 3-inch discs. Brush one side of each of these with jam and stick to the front of the cakes. Roll out the untinted icing and using the cookie cutter, stamp out 12 crescents for Santa's beard. Brush one side of each crescent with cold water and stick to the bottom half of Santa's face. Cut out mustaches and stick above the beard. Fill the piping bag with Meringue Buttercream and pipe a swirl on top of each cake. Sit the Santa hat on top of this. Pipe a ruffle around the bottom of the hat and a snowball bobble on the top. Give Santa a red icing nose and eyes with 2 blobs of untinted fondant and dots of black food coloring paste.

Look out for pretty, feathered bird ornaments to perch on top of these cakes. I have used robins but if you're lucky you may spot some really special, sparkly exotic birds in the shops at this time of year.

flock of robins

1 quantity Double Chocolate Cake (page 8)

1 quantity Chocolate Meringue Buttercream (page 9)

12 short chocolate flake bars

confectioners' sugar, for dusting

1–2 muffin pans, lined with 12 brown paper cupcake liners

12 feathered robins

makes 12

Preheat the oven to 350°F.

Divide the Double Chocolate Cake between the cupcake liners, filling them two-thirds full.

Bake on the middle shelf of the preheated oven for about 20 minutes, or until well risen and a skewer inserted into the middle of the cakes comes out clean. Remove from the oven and let cool in the pan for 5 minutes before transferring to a wire rack to cool completely.

Spread the Chocolate Meringue Buttercream generously onto each cold cupcake. Sit a chocolate flake in the middle of each cake, perch a robin on top, and dust with confectioners' sugar.

Almost too cute to eat, these fine fellows are bursting with character and charm. Have fun with their accessories and expressions to give them each their own personality. Sprinkle desiccated coconut all around them to create a snowy scene.

snow-ho-ho-men

2½ oz. natural marzipan

orange food coloring paste

black food coloring paste

1 quantity Buttermilk Cake (page 8)

1 quantity Marshmallow Frosting (page 9)

10 oz. desiccated coconut

16–20 colored sugar-coated candies

8–10 large chocolate buttons

licorice sticks, cut into 8–10 x ½-inch lengths

muffin pan, lined with 8–10 paper or silver cupcake liners

mini-muffin pan, lined with 8–10 paper or silver liners in the coordinating size

8–10 toothpicks

narrow festive ribbon, cut into 8–10 x 10-inch lengths

makes 8–10

Make the noses, mouths, and eyes the day before you make the snowmen. Tint three-quarters of the marzipan orange using the food coloring paste. Break off small nuggets of the marzipan and roll into carrot shapes. Tint the remaining marzipan black and roll into tiny balls, allowing roughly 4 for each snowman's mouth and 1 for each eye. Set aside on baking parchment in an airtight box to dry out overnight.

The next day, preheat the oven to 350°F.

Divide the Buttermilk Cake between the paper liners, filling them two-thirds full. Bake on the middle shelf of the preheated oven for 12–25 minutes, depending on the size of the cakes—take them out when they are well risen and a skewer inserted into the middle of the cakes comes out clean. Remove from the oven and let cool in the pan for 5 minutes before transferring to a wire rack to cool completely.

Spread the Marshmallow Frosting onto each cold cupcake, right to the edge. Scatter the desiccated coconut over the top. Press the marzipan noses into the middle of each smaller cake and arrange the tiny black marzipan balls as the eyes and mouths. Press the sugar-coated candies down the middle of each larger cupcake to make buttons. To make the hats, dab a tiny amount of frosting in the middle of each chocolate button and stick the licorice onto it. Lay each large cupcake on its side with the coconut facing you and the buttons in a vertical line. Carefully push a toothpick into what is now the top of each cake so that there is still 1 inch of the toothpick exposed. Push a mini-muffin onto the toothpick to make the head. Tie a length of ribbon around the neck of each snowman and balance the hat on top of his head.

I have topped these spiced cakes with white iced doves but feel free to make the gingerbread cookies in whatever shape you like—snowmen, stars, and trees would all work well.

gingerbread doves
on gingerbread cupcakes

1 quantity Sticky Gingerbread cupcakes (page 24)

1 quantity Meringue Buttercream (page 9)

2 tablespoons chopped stem ginger in syrup

1 teaspoon ground cinnamon

gingerbread cookie doves

1 stick unsalted butter, softened

⅓ cup packed dark brown sugar

1 egg, beaten

6 tablespoons honey

2¾ cups all-purpose flour, plus extra for dusting

½ teaspoon baking powder

1 teaspoon baking soda

2 teaspoons apple pie spice

3 teaspoons ground ginger

a pinch of salt

1½ cups royal icing mix

dove-shaped cookie cutter

1–2 baking sheets, lined with baking parchment

makes 12

To make the gingerbread cookie doves, cream together the butter and sugar until light and fluffy. Add the beaten egg and honey and mix until smooth. Sift together the flour, baking powder, baking soda, spices, and salt. Add to the egg mixture and mix until smooth. Knead the dough lightly—just enough to bring it together—then wrap in plastic wrap and refrigerate for a couple of hours until firm.

Preheat the oven to 350°F.

Meanwhile, make and bake the Sticky Gingerbread cupcakes as described on page 24. Leave the oven on.

Lightly dust a clean, dry work surface with all-purpose flour. Roll the chilled cookie dough out to a thickness of ⅛ inch. Using the dove cookie cutter, stamp out 12 shapes. Place on the prepared baking sheets and bake on the middle shelf of the preheated oven for 12 minutes, or until firm. Remove from the oven and let cool on the sheets for 5 minutes before transferring to a wire rack to cool completely.

Make the royal icing according to the package instructions and spread over the cold cookie doves with a small palette knife. Let set for a couple of hours.

Put the Meringue Buttercream in a bowl and stir in the stem ginger and cinnamon. Spread the frosting generously onto each cold cupcake, then perch a dove on top.

These cupcakes are adorable, and can be adapted to any color scheme you like. The stockings are made from marzipan (or sugar paste, if you prefer), so tint it the right shade by gradually adding more coloring paste and kneading it in.

christmas stockings

10 oz. natural marzipan (or sugar paste, if you prefer)

red food coloring paste

1 quantity Buttermilk or Double Chocolate Cake (page 8)

red, green, and white sprinkles

1 quantity Vanilla Buttercream (page 9)

12 sugar snowflakes

1–2 muffin pans, lined with 12 paper cupcake liners

makes 12

Make the stockings at least a day before you plan to serve the cupcakes. Tint the marzipan red using the food coloring paste. Shape the colored marzipan into stockings. Set aside on baking parchment in an airtight box to dry out overnight.

The next day, preheat the oven to 350°F.

Divide the Buttermilk or Double Chocolate Cake between the paper liners, filling them two-thirds full.

Bake on the middle shelf of the preheated oven for about 20 minutes, or until well risen and a skewer inserted into the middle of the cakes comes out clean. Remove from the oven and let cool in the pan for 5 minutes before transferring to a wire rack to cool completely.

Mix the red, green, and white sprinkles in a bowl. Spread the Vanilla Buttercream generously onto each cold cupcake. Dip the edges of the cupcakes into the mixed sprinkles and top with a marzipan stocking. Stick a sugar snowflake onto each stocking with a dab of buttercream.

decorative

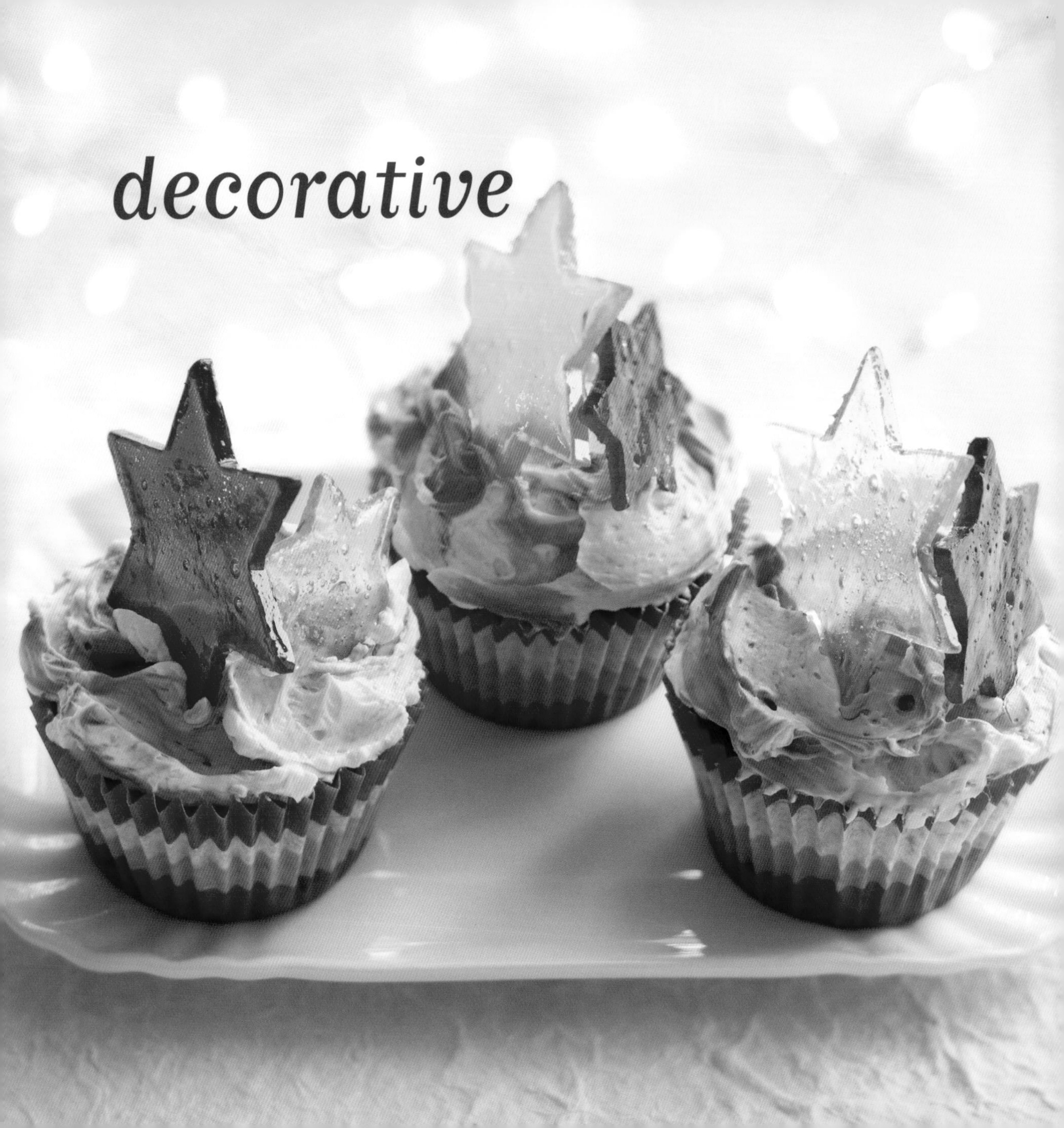

You can make these ultra-pretty but very easy hard-candy stars in advance—just don't arrange on top of the frosted cupcakes until just before serving.

stained-glass stars

1 quantity Buttermilk Cake
(page 8)

assorted hard candies,
such as Jolly Rancher

1 quantity Meringue
Buttercream (page 9)

red food coloring paste

1–2 muffin pans, lined with
12–16 paper cupcake liners

star-shaped cookie cutters in
assorted sizes, well oiled

baking sheet,
lined with baking parchment

makes 12–16

Preheat the oven to 350°F.

Divide the Buttermilk Cake between the cupcake liners, filling them two-thirds full.

Bake on the middle shelf of the preheated oven for about 20 minutes, or until golden, well risen, and a skewer inserted into the middle of the cakes comes out clean. Remove from the oven (leaving the oven on) and let cool in the pan for 5 minutes before transferring to a wire rack to cool completely.

To make the stained-glass stars, unwrap the candies and separate them by color. Place each color in its own freezer bag and crush with a rolling pin. Arrange the well-oiled cookie cutters on the prepared baking sheet. Fill each cutter with a thin layer of one color of crushed candies. Bake on the middle shelf of the hot oven for about 5 minutes, or until melted. Let the stars cool on the parchment paper for about 5 minutes before popping out of their cutters. Repeat with the remaining candies.

Divide the Meringue Buttercream between two bowls and tint one red using the food coloring paste. Using a large metal spoon, very lightly stir one color into the other so that they become marbled. Spread generously onto each cold cupcake and create messy peaks with the back of a spoon. Stand 2 or 3 stained-glass stars in the frosting.

You will need to make two batches of cupcakes for this idea so that you have 24 cupcakes to represent the Advent season. The numbers should be made 2 days in advance of serving so that they have time to dry before assembling.

advent cupcakes

1 lb. white ready-to-roll fondant or royal icing

blue food coloring paste

confectioners' sugar, for dusting

2 quantities Buttermilk Cake (page 8) or Red Velvet cupcakes (page 28)

2 quantities Meringue Buttercream (page 9)

edible white and/or blue glitter

small, numbered cutters

small square and round cutters

2–4 muffin pans, lined with 24 festive paper cupcake liners

large piping bag, fitted with a star tip

makes 24

Make the fondant/royal-icing numbers 2 days before you make the cupcakes. Divide the icing into two. Tint half of it pale blue using the food coloring paste and leave the other half untinted. Lightly dust a clean, dry work surface with confectioners' sugar. Roll the icing out to a thickness of no more than 1/16 inch. Using the square and round cutters, stamp out 24 shapes. Then stamp out numbers 1–24 to represent the days of Advent. Lightly brush the underside of each number with a dab of cold water and stick to the squares and circles. Set aside on baking parchment to dry out for 2 days.

When you are ready to make the cupcakes, preheat the oven to 350°F.

Divide the Buttermilk Cake or Red Velvet cupcakes between the cupcake liners, filling them two-thirds full.

Bake on the middle shelf of the preheated oven for about 20 minutes, or until well risen and a skewer inserted into the middle of the cakes comes out clean. Remove from the oven and let cool in the pan for 5 minutes before transferring to a wire rack to cool completely.

Fill the piping bag with the Meringue Buttercream and pipe generous swirls onto each cold cupcake. Dust with white and/or blue glitter. Let set for 30 minutes. Meanwhile, scatter more glitter on a small plate. Dab a little cold water around the edges of the numbered shapes and dip them in the glitter before pushing into the set buttercream on each cupcake.

Keep an eye out for sets of holly leaf cutters in assorted sizes and make a selection of fondant- or royal-icing leaves to top each cupcake. Keep the cupcake liners plain or buy matching, decorative ones to make the cupcakes extra special.

holly leaves & berries

10 oz. white ready-to-roll fondant or royal icing

green food coloring paste

confectioners' sugar, for dusting

edible green glitter

1 quantity Red Velvet cupcakes (page 28)

1 quantity Marshmallow Frosting (page 9)

red, green, and white sprinkles

red sugar balls

holly-shaped cutters in assorted sizes

1–2 muffin pans, lined with 12 festive paper cupcake liners

makes 12

Make the fondant/royal-icing holly leaves 2 days before you make the cupcakes. Tint the icing green using the food coloring paste. Lightly dust a clean, dry work surface with confectioners' sugar. Roll the icing out to a thickness of no more than $\frac{1}{16}$ inch. Using the assorted holly cutters, stamp out as many shapes as you like. Use the blunt side of a knife or a skewer to mark veins in each leaf, then dust with edible green glitter. Set aside on baking parchment to dry out for 2 days.

When you are ready to make the cupcakes, preheat the oven to 350°F.

Make and bake the Red Velvet cupcakes as described on page 28.

Mix the red, green, and white sprinkles in a bowl. Spread the Marshmallow Frosting generously onto each cold cupcake. Dip the edges of the cupcakes into the mixed sprinkles. Top with the holly leaves and red sugar balls.

Bake these cakes in adorable mini-cupcake liners, package into pretty boxes, and prepare to pucker up under the mistletoe! They make an irresistible gift for someone special.

mistletoe mini-cupcakes

2 oz. white ready-to-roll fondant or royal icing
green food coloring paste
1 stick unsalted butter, softened
½ cup plus 2 tablespoons sugar
2 eggs, beaten
1 teaspoon pure vanilla extract
1 cup all-purpose flour
2 teaspoons baking powder
a pinch of salt
½ quantity Marshmallow Frosting (page 9)
white sprinkles
white pearly sugar balls

mini-muffin pan, lined with 18 paper liners in the coordinating size

makes 18

Make the sprigs of mistletoe 2 days before you make the cupcakes. Tint the fondant/royal icing green using the food coloring paste. Break off nuggets of the icing and shape into mistletoe stalks and leaves. Use the blunt side of a knife or a skewer to mark veins in each leaf. Set aside on baking parchment to dry out for 2 days.

When you are ready to make the cupcakes, preheat the oven to 350°F.

Cream together the butter and sugar until light and creamy. Gradually add the beaten eggs, mixing well between each addition and scraping down the side of the mixing bowl from time to time. Add the vanilla. Sift together the flour, baking powder, and salt and stir into the egg mixture, beating until smooth and thoroughly combined. Divide the mixture between the cupcake liners, filling them two-thirds full.

Bake on the middle shelf of the preheated oven for 12–15 minutes, or until golden, well risen, and a skewer inserted into the middle of the cakes comes out clean. Remove from the oven and let cool in the pan for 5 minutes before transferring to a wire rack to cool completely.

Spread the Marshmallow Frosting generously onto each cold cupcake. Scatter white sprinkles over the frosting, then top with a mistletoe sprig and 2 or 3 white pearly sugar balls, for berries.

I have used a light fruit cake recipe to make these little cupcake gifts. Tint the icing whatever color you like for your gift wrapping but I think the cakes look more sophisticated with a simple color scheme such as red and white.

fruit cake gifts
with marzipan

14 oz. white ready-to-roll fondant icing

red food coloring paste

confectioners' sugar, for dusting

4 tablespoons apricot jam

10 oz. natural marzipan

fruit cake

1½ sticks unsalted butter, softened

¾ cup sugar

3 eggs, beaten

1 cup plus 2 tablespoons all-purpose flour

3 teaspoons baking powder

½ teaspoon ground cinnamon

a pinch of grated nutmeg

a pinch of salt

2 tablespoons ground almonds

⅔ cup mixed raisins

⅓ cup glacé cherries, chopped

2 tablespoons candied peel, finely chopped

grated peel and juice of ½ orange

1–2 muffin pans, lined with 12 red paper cupcake liners

round cookie cutter, same diameter as top of cupcakes

makes 12

Preheat the oven to 350°F.

To make the fruit cake, cream together the butter and sugar until light and fluffy. Gradually add the beaten eggs, mixing well between each addition and scraping down the bowl from time to time with a rubber spatula. Sift together the flour, baking powder, spices, and salt. Add to the egg mixture with the ground almonds and mix until just combined. Add the dried fruits, orange peel, and juice and mix until smooth. Divide the mixture between the paper liners, filling them two-thirds full. Bake on the middle shelf of the preheated oven for about 20 minutes, or until golden, well risen, and a skewer inserted into the middle of the cakes comes out clean. Remove from the oven and let cool in the pan for 5 minutes before transferring to a wire rack to cool completely.

Tint half the fondant icing red using the food coloring paste, wrap in plastic wrap, and set aside. Lightly dust a clean, dry work surface with confectioners' sugar. Roll the marzipan out to a thickness of 1/16 inch. Using the cookie cutter, stamp out 12 discs. Warm the apricot jam in a small saucepan, sieve it, then lightly brush the tops of the cold cupcakes. Press one marzipan disc onto the top of each cake, smoothing to cover the cake completely. Brush the marzipan with another thin layer of apricot jam. Roll out the untinted fondant icing (slightly thicker than the marzipan) and stamp out 12 discs using the cutter. Use them to cover the marzipan-topped cakes and smooth down.

Roll out the red fondant, cut into strips, lightly brush with water, and lay across the top of each cupcake to resemble ribbons. Arrange more strips into bows and stick to the cakes with a dab of water.

This has to be one of the prettiest ways to decorate a festive cupcake and as it only requires a star piping tip, it's one of the simplest too. If you don't fancy piping a ribbon on each wreath you can tie a thin ribbon into a bow instead.

christmas wreaths

1 quantity Buttermilk or Double Chocolate Cake (page 8) or Red Velvet cupcakes (page 28)

1 quantity Meringue Buttercream (page 9)

green food coloring paste

red food coloring paste

1–2 muffin pans, lined with 12 green paper cupcake liners

large piping bag, fitted with a star tip

small piping bag, fitted with a writing tip

makes 12

Preheat the oven to 350°F.

Divide the Buttermilk or Chocolate Cake, or Red Velvet cupcakes between the cupcake liners, filling them two-thirds full.

Bake on the middle shelf of the preheated oven for about 20 minutes, or until well risen and a skewer inserted into the middle of the cakes comes out clean. Remove from the oven and let cool in the pan for 5 minutes before transferring to a wire rack to cool completely.

Spoon one-third of the Meringue Buttercream into a bowl and tint green using the food coloring paste. Put another 2 tablespoons into another, small bowl, and tint red. Leave the remainder untinted.

Spread the untinted frosting generously onto each cold cupcake. Take the piping bag with the star tip and fill with the green frosting. Pipe small rosettes in a wreath shape on top of each cake. Fill the piping bag with the writing tip with the red frosting and pipe small red berries around the wreath, and a ribbon at the top.

You'll need to buy star-shaped cutters to make these icing stars, then let the stars dry out for 2 days before serving. Keep an eye out for laser-cut cupcake wrappers in good bakeware stores or from online suppliers to complete the starry theme.

catch a falling star

confectioners' sugar, for dusting

1 lb. white ready-to-roll fondant or royal icing

gold and silver luster dusts

1 quantity Buttermilk or Double Chocolate Cake (page 8)

1 quantity Marshmallow Frosting (page 9)

edible gold glitter

edible gold star sprinkles

star-shaped cutters in assorted sizes

1–2 muffin pans, lined with 12 paper cupcake liners

large piping bag, fitted with a large star tip

12 laser-cut cupcake wrappers (optional)

makes 12

Make the fondant/royal-icing stars 2 days before you make the cupcakes. Lightly dust a clean, dry work surface with confectioners' sugar. Roll the icing out to a thickness of no more than 1/16 inch. Using the assorted star cutters, stamp out as many shapes as you like. Set aside on baking parchment to dry out for 2 days.

When you are ready to make the cupcakes, preheat the oven to 350°F.

Dust the fondant-icing stars with gold or silver luster dust.

Divide the Buttermilk or Double Chocolate Cake between the cupcake liners, filling them two-thirds full.

Bake on the middle shelf of the preheated oven for about 20 minutes, or until well risen and a skewer inserted into the middle of the cakes comes out clean. Remove from the oven and let cool in the pan for 5 minutes before transferring to a wire rack to cool completely.

Fill the piping bag with the Marshmallow Frosting and pipe generous swirls onto each cold cupcake. Sprinkle with a flurry of gold glitter and star sprinkles, and finish with a stack of icing stars. Finally, wrap a cupcake wrapper around each cupcake, if using.

There really is no limit to how decorative you can be with these cakes and with the wide range of luster dust, glitter, and food colors now available, the sky's the limit! You can also use embossing tools to create pretty patterns over each ornament.

christmas ornaments
with marzipan

1 quantity Buttermilk Cake (page 8)

14 oz. white ready-to-roll fondant icing

assorted food coloring pastes

confectioners' sugar, for dusting

10 oz. natural marzipan

4 tablespoons apricot jam

assorted edible luster dusts

1½ cups royal icing mix

edible colored balls

1–2 muffin pans, lined with 12 paper cupcake liners

round cookie cutter, same diameter as top of cupcakes

small piping bags, fitted with writing tips

narrow festive ribbon (optional)

makes 12

Preheat the oven to 350°F.

Divide the Buttermilk Cake between the cupcake liners, filling them two-thirds full.

Bake on the middle shelf of the preheated oven for about 20 minutes, or until golden, well risen, and a skewer inserted into the middle of the cakes comes out clean. Remove from the oven and let cool in the pan for 5 minutes before transferring to a wire rack to cool completely.

Break off about 2½ oz. of the fondant icing, wrap in plastic wrap, and set aside. Tint the remaining fondant in your chosen colors. Cover with plastic wrap until ready to use. Lightly dust a clean, dry work surface with confectioners' sugar. Roll the marzipan out to a thickness of ⅟₁₆ inch. Using the cookie cutter, stamp out 12 discs. Warm the apricot jam in a small saucepan, sieve it, then lightly brush the tops of the cold cupcakes. Press one marzipan disc onto the top of each cake, smoothing to cover the cake completely. Brush the marzipan with another thin layer of apricot jam. Roll out the tinted fondant icing (slightly thicker than the marzipan) and stamp out 12 discs using the cutter. Cover the marzipan-topped cakes and smooth down. Brush luster dusts lightly over the fondant.

Make the royal icing according to the package instructions and tint in your chosen colors. Fill the piping bags with the icing and pipe designs onto each ornament. Decorate with colored balls. Use the reserved untinted fondant to make little loops, brush each one with luster dust, and press into the top of each ornament. Finish with ribbon.

These beautiful cupcakes are topped with a snowdrift of marshmallow frosting. Make the sugar-paste snowflakes a couple of days before serving and let dry before decorating with royal icing and assorted sprinkles and glitter.

flurry of snowflakes

confectioners' sugar, for dusting

8 oz. white sugar paste

⅔ cup royal icing mix

edible silver and white glitter and/or luster dust

1 quantity Buttermilk Cake (page 8) but with ⅔ cup chocolate chips stirred in at the end

white sprinkles

1 quantity Marshmallow Frosting (page 9)

small snowflake-shaped cutter

1–2 muffin pans, lined with 12 paper cupcake liners

small piping bag, fitted with a writing tip

makes 12

Make the sugar-paste snowflakes the day before you make the cupcakes. Lightly dust a clean, dry work surface with confectioners' sugar. Roll the sugar paste out to a thickness of no more than ⅟₁₆ inch. Using the snowflake cutter, stamp out 12 snowflakes. Set aside on baking parchment to dry out overnight.

The next day, make the royal icing according to the package instructions. Fill the piping bag with the icing and pipe little dots onto the sugar-paste snowflakes. Sprinkle with edible glitter and/or luster dust and let set.

When you are ready to make the cupcakes, preheat the oven to 350°F.

Divide the Buttermilk Cake between the cupcake liners, filling them two-thirds full.

Bake on the middle shelf of the preheated oven for about 20 minutes, or until golden, well risen, and a skewer inserted into the middle of the cakes comes out clean. Remove from the oven and let cool in the pan for 5 minutes before transferring to a wire rack to cool completely.

Put the white sprinkles in a bowl. Spread the Marshmallow Frosting generously onto each cold cupcake. Finish with a little flourish at the top. Dip the edges of the cupcakes into the sprinkles and dust with more glitter and/or luster dust. Top with a sugar-paste snowflake.

A batch of these decorative miniature poinsettias would make an original centerpiece on a Christmas dinner table. Why not admire them during the meal, and then enjoy them for dessert!

candle-lit poinsettias

10 oz. white ready-to-roll fondant or royal icing

red food coloring paste

confectioners' sugar, for dusting

1 quantity Buttermilk or Double Chocolate Cake (page 8)

1 quantity Meringue Buttercream (page 9)

green food coloring paste

yellow food coloring paste

assorted small flower-shaped cutters

1–2 muffin pans, lined with 12 paper cupcake liners

small piping bag, fitted with a leaf tip

12 small candles and holders

makes 12

Make the fondant/royal-icing flowers 2 days before you make the cupcakes. Tint the icing red using the food coloring paste. Lightly dust a clean, dry work surface with confectioners' sugar. Roll the icing out to a thickness of no more than 1⁄16 inch. Using the assorted flower cutters, stamp out the required number of shapes—you will need about 9 for each cupcake. Set aside on baking parchment to dry out for 2 days.

When you are ready to make the cupcakes, preheat the oven to 350°F.

Divide the Buttermilk or Double Chocolate Cake between the cupcake liners, filling them two-thirds full.

Bake on the middle shelf of the preheated oven for about 20 minutes, or until well risen and a skewer inserted into the middle of the cakes comes out clean. Remove from the oven and let cool in the pan for 5 minutes before transferring to a wire rack to cool completely.

Spoon 6 tablespoons of the Meringue Buttercream into a small bowl and tint green using the food coloring paste. Fill the piping bag with the frosting. In another small bowl, transfer another tablespoon of frosting and tint it yellow.

Spread the remaining, untinted frosting generously onto each cold cupcake. Using the green frosting, pipe small leaves around the edge of each cupcake. Push a candle, in its holder, in the middle of each cake. Arrange the poinsettias around it and dab a dot of yellow frosting in the center of each one.

index

conversion chart

The recipes in this book require the following conversions. Please note that weights and measures have been rounded up or down to make measuring easier.

Measuring butter:

A US stick of butter weighs 4 oz. which is approximately 115 g or 8 tablespoons.

American	Metric	Imperial
1 tbsp	85 g	3 oz.
7 tbsp	100 g	3½ oz.
1 stick	115 g	4 oz.

Volume equivalents:

American	Metric	Imperial
1 teaspoon	5 ml	
1 tablespoon	15 ml	
¼ cup	60 ml	2 fl.oz.
⅓ cup	75 ml	2½ fl.oz.
½ cup	125 ml	4 fl.oz.
⅔ cup	150 ml	5 fl.oz. (¼ pint)
¾ cup	175 ml	6 fl.oz.
1 cup	250 ml	8 fl.oz.

Weight equivalents:		Measurements:	
Imperial	Metric	Inches	Cm
1 oz.	30 g	¼ inch	0.5 cm
2 oz.	55 g	½ inch	1 cm
3 oz.	85 g	¾ inch	1.5 cm
3½ oz.	100 g	1 inch	2.5 cm
4 oz.	115 g	2 inches	5 cm
5 oz.	140 g	3 inches	7 cm
6 oz.	175 g	4 inches	10 cm
8 oz. (½ lb.)	225 g	5 inches	12 cm
9 oz.	250 g	6 inches	15 cm
10 oz.	280 g	7 inches	18 cm
11½ oz.	325 g	8 inches	20 cm
12 oz.	350 g	9 inches	23 cm
13 oz.	375 g	10 inches	25 cm
14 oz.	400 g	11 inches	28 cm
15 oz.	425 g	12 inches	30 cm
16 oz. (1 lb.)	450 g		

Oven temperatures:

160°C	(325°F)	Gas 3
180°C	(350°F)	Gas 4